The London Baptist Confession of Faith

1689

Layout and design: copyright @ Icthus press, 2015.

Ed.. P.Moore

Table of Contents

Chapter 1: Of the Holy Scriptures

1)   The Holy Scripture is the only sufficient, certain, and infallible rule of all saving knowledge, faith, and obedience, although the light of nature, and the works of creation and providence do so far manifest the goodness, wisdom, and power of God, as to leave men inexcusable; yet are they not sufficient to give that knowledge of God and his will which is necessary unto salvation.

Therefore it pleased the Lord at sundry times and in divers manners to reveal himself, and to declare that his will unto his church; and afterward for the better preserving and propagating of the truth, and for the more sure establishment and comfort of the church against the corruption of the flesh, and the malice of Satan, and of the world, to commit the same wholly unto writing; which maketh the Holy Scriptures to be most necessary, those former ways of God's revealing his will unto his people being now ceased

. (2 Timothy 3:15-17; Isaiah 8:20; Luke 16:29, 31; Ephesians 2:20; Romans 1:19-21; Romans 2:14,15; Psalms 19:1-3; Hebrews 1:1; Proverbs 22:19-21; Romans 15:4; 2 Peter 1:19,20)

2).   Under the name of Holy Scripture, or the Word of God written, are now contained all the books of the Old and New Testaments, which are these:

OF THE OLD TESTAMENT: *Genesis, Exodus, Leviticus, Numbers, Deuteronomy, Joshua, Judges, Ruth, I Samuel, II*

Samuel, I Kings, II Kings, I Chronicles, II Chronicles, Ezra, Nehemiah, Esther, Job, Psalms, Proverbs, Ecclesiastes, The Song of Solomen, Isaiah, Jeremiah, Lamentations,Ezekiel, Daniel, Hosea, Joel, Amos, Obadiah, Jonah, Micah, Nahum, Habakkuk, Zephaniah, Haggai, Zechariah, Malachi

OF THE NEW TESTAMENT: *Matthew, Mark, Luke, John, The Acts of the Apostles, Paul's Epistle to the Romans, I Corinthians, II Corinthians, Galatians, Ephesians, Philippians, Colossians, I Thessalonians, II Thessalonians, I Timothy, II Timothy, To Titus, To Philemon, The Epistle to the Hebrews, Epistle of James, The first and second Epistles of Peter, The first, second, and third Epistles of John, The Epistle of Jude, The Revelation*

All of which are given by the inspiration of God, to be the rule of faith and life. (2 Timothy 3:16)

3).   The books commonly called Apocrypha, not being of divine inspiration, are no part of the canon or rule of the Scripture, and, therefore, are of no authority to the church of God, nor to be any otherwise approved or made use of than other human writings.
(Luke 24:27, 44; Romans 3:2)

4).   The authority of the Holy Scripture, for which it ought to be believed, dependeth not upon the testimony of any man or church, but wholly upon God (who is truth itself), the author thereof; therefore it is to be received because it is the Word of God.
(2 Peter 1:19-21; 2 Timothy 3:16; 2 Thessalonians 2:13; 1 John 5:9)

5). We may be moved and induced by the testimony of the church of God to an high and reverent esteem of the Holy Scriptures; and the heavenliness of the matter, the efficacy of the doctrine, and the majesty of the style, the consent of all the parts, the scope of the whole (which is to give all glory to God), the full discovery it makes of the only way of man's salvation, and many other incomparable excellencies, and entire perfections thereof, are arguments whereby it doth abundantly evidence itself to be the Word of God; yet notwithstanding, our full persuasion and assurance of the infallible truth, and divine authority thereof, is from the inward work of the Holy Spirit bearing witness by and with the Word in our hearts.
(John 16:13,14; 1 Corinthians 2:10-12; 1 John 2:20, 27)

6). The whole counsel of God concerning all things necessary for his own glory, man's salvation, faith and life, is either expressly set down or necessarily contained in the Holy Scripture: unto which nothing at any time is to be added, whether by new revelation of the Spirit, or traditions of men. Nevertheless, we acknowledge the inward illumination of the Spirit of God to be necessary for the saving understanding of such things as are revealed in the Word, and that there are some circumstances concerning the worship of God, and government of the church, common to human actions and societies, which are to be ordered by the light of nature and Christian prudence, according to the general rules of the Word, which are always to be observed.

(2 Timothy 3:15-17; Galatians 1:8,9; John 6:45; 1 Corinthians 2:9-12; 1 Corinthians 11:13, 14; 1 Corinthians 14:26,40)

7). All things in Scripture are not alike plain in themselves, nor alike clear unto all; yet those things which are necessary to be known, believed and observed for salvation, are so clearly propounded and opened in some place of Scripture or other, that not only the learned, but the unlearned, in a due use of ordinary means, may attain to a sufficient understanding of them.

(2 Peter 3:16; Psalms 19:7; Psalms 119:130)

8). The Old Testament in Hebrew (which was the native language of the people of God of old), and the New Testament in Greek (which at the time of the writing of it was most generally known to the nations), being immediately inspired by God, and by his singular care and providence kept pure in all ages, are therefore authentic; so as in all controversies of religion, the church is finally to appeal to them. But because these original tongues are not known to all the people of God, who have a right unto, and interest in the Scriptures, and are commanded in the fear of God to read and search them, therefore they are to be translated into the vulgar language of every nation unto which they come, that the Word of God dwelling plentifully in all, they may worship him in an acceptable manner, and through patience and comfort of the Scriptures may have hope. (Romans 3:2; Isaiah 8:20; Acts 15:15; John 5:39; 1 Corinthians 14:6, 9, 11, 12, 24, 28; Colossians 3:16)

9). The infallible rule of interpretation of Scripture is the Scripture itself; and therefore when there is a question about the true and full sense of any Scripture (which is not manifold, but one), it must be searched by other places that speak more clearly.

(2 Peter 1:20, 21; Acts 15:15, 16)

10).   The supreme judge, by which all controversies of religion are to be determined, and all decrees of councils, opinions of ancient writers, doctrines of men, and private spirits, are to be examined, and in whose sentence we are to rest, can be no other but the Holy Scripture delivered by the Spirit, into which Scripture so delivered, our faith is finally resolved.
(Matthew 22:29, 31, 32; Ephesians 2:20; Acts 28:23)

Chapter 2: Of God and of the Holy Trinity

1).   The Lord our God is but one only living and true God; whose subsistence is in and of himself, infinite in being and perfection; whose essence cannot be comprehended by any but himself; a most pure spirit, invisible, without body, parts, or passions, who only hath immortality, dwelling in the light which no man can approach unto; who is immutable, immense, eternal, incomprehensible, almighty, every way infinite, most holy, most wise, most free, most absolute; working all things according to the counsel of his own immutable and most righteous will for his own glory; most loving, gracious, merciful, long-suffering, abundant in goodness and truth, forgiving iniquity, transgression, and sin; the rewarder of them that diligently seek him, and withal most just and terrible in his judgments, hating all sin, and who will by no means clear the guilty.
(1 Corinthians 8:4, 6; Deuteronomy 6:4; Jeremiah 10:10; Isaiah 48:12; Exodus 3:14; John 4:24; 1 Timothy 1:17; Deuteronomy 4:15, 16; Malachi 3:6; 1 Kings 8:27; Jeremiah 23:23; Psalms 90:2; Genesis 17:1; Isaiah 6:3; Psalms 115:3; Isaiah 46:10; Proverbs 16:4; Romans 11:36; Exodus 34:6, 7; Hebrews 11:6; Nehemiah 9:32, 33; Psalms 5:5, 6; Exodus 34:7; Nahum 1:2, 3)

2).   God, having all life, glory, goodness, blessedness, in and of himself, is alone in and unto himself all-sufficient, not standing in need of any creature which he hath made, nor deriving any glory from them, but only manifesting his own glory in, by, unto, and upon them; he is the alone fountain of

all being, of whom, through whom, and to whom are all things, and he hath most sovereign dominion over all creatures, to do by them, for them,
or upon them, whatsoever himself pleaseth; in his sight all things are open and manifest, his knowledge is infinite, infallible, and independent upon the creature, so as nothing is to him contingent or uncertain; he is most holy in all his counsels, in all his works, and in all his commands; to him is due from angels and men, whatsoever worship, service, or obedience, as creatures they owe unto the Creator, and whatever he is further pleased to require of them.
(John 5:26; Psalms 148:13; Psalms 119:68; Job 22:2, 3; Romans 11:34-36; Daniel 4:25, 34, 35; Hebrews 4:13; Ezekiel 11:5; Acts 15:18; Psalms 145:17; Revelation 5:12-14)

3).   In this divine and infinite Being there are three subsistences, the Father, the Word or Son, and Holy Spirit, of one substance, power, and eternity, each having the whole divine essence, yet the essence undivided: the Father is of none, neither begotten nor proceeding; the Son is eternally begotten of the Father; the Holy Spirit proceeding from the Father and the Son; all infinite, without beginning, therefore but one God, who is not to be divided in nature and being, but distinguished by several peculiar relative properties and personal relations; which doctrine of the Trinity is the foundation of all our communion with God, and comfortable dependence on him.
(1 John 5:7; Matthew 28:19; 2 Corinthians 13:14; Exodus 3:14; John 14:11; 1 Corinthians 8:6; John 1:14,18; John 15:26; Galatians 4:6)

Chapter 3:Of God's Decree

1)   God hath decreed in himself, from all eternity, by the most wise and holy counsel of his own will, freely and unchangeably, all things, whatsoever comes to pass; yet so as thereby is God neither the author of sin nor hath fellowship with any therein; nor is violence offered to the will of the creature, nor yet is the liberty or contingency of second causes taken away, but rather established; in which appears his wisdom in disposing all things, and power and faithfulness in accomplishing his decree.

(Isaiah 46:10; Ephesians 1:11; Hebrews 6:17; Romans 9:15, 18; James 1:13; 1 John 1:5; Acts 4:27, 28; John 19:11; Numbers 23:19; Ephesians 1:3-5)

2)   Although God knoweth whatsoever may or can come to pass, upon all supposed conditions, yet hath he not decreed anything, because he foresaw it as future, or as that which would come to pass upon such conditions.

(Acts 15:18; Romans 9:11, 13, 16, 18)

3)   By the decree of God, for the manifestation of his glory, some men and angels are predestinated, or foreordained to eternal life through Jesus Christ, to the praise of his glorious grace; others being left to act in their sin to their just condemnation, to the praise of his glorious justice.

(1 Timothy 5:21; Matthew 25:34; Ephesians 1:5, 6; Romans 9:22, 23; Jude 4)

4)   These angels and men thus predestinated and foreordained, are particularly and unchangeably designed, and their number so certain and definite, that it cannot be either increased or diminished.

(2 Timothy 2:19; John 13:18)

5)   Those of mankind that are predestinated to life, God, before the foundation of the world was laid, according to his eternal and immutable purpose, and the secret counsel and good pleasure of his will, hath chosen in Christ unto everlasting glory, out of his mere free grace and love, without any other thing in the creature as a condition or cause moving him thereunto.

(Ephesians 1:4, 9, 11; Romans 8:30; 2 Timothy 1:9; 1 Thessalonians 5:9; Romans 9:13, 16; Ephesians 2:5, 12)

6)   As God hath appointed the elect unto glory, so he hath, by the eternal and most free purpose of his will, foreordained all the means thereunto; wherefore they who are elected, being fallen in Adam, are redeemed by Christ, are effectually called unto faith in Christ, by his Spirit working in due season, are justified, adopted, sanctified, and kept by his power through faith unto salvation; neither are any other redeemed by Christ, or effectually called, justified, adopted, sanctified, and saved, but the elect only.

(1 Peter 1:2; 2 Thessalonians 2:13; 1 Thessalonians 5:9, 10; Romans 8:30; 2 Thessalonians 2:13; 1 Peter 1:5; John 10:26; John 17:9; John 6:64)

7)   The doctrine of the high mystery of predestination is to be handled with special prudence and care, that men attending the will of God revealed in his Word, and yielding

obedience thereunto, may, from the certainty of their effectual vocation, be assured of their eternal election; so shall this doctrine afford matter of praise, reverence, and admiration of God, and of humility, diligence, and abundant consolation to all that sincerely obey the gospel.

(1 Thessalonians 1:4, 5; 2 Peter 1:10; Ephesians 1:6; Romans 11:33; Romans 11:5, 6, 20; Luke 10:20)

Chapter 4:Of Creation

1)   In the beginning it pleased God the Father, Son, and Holy Spirit, for the manifestation of the glory of his eternal power, wisdom, and goodness, to create or make the world, and all things therein, whether visible or invisible, in the space of six days, and all very good.

(John 1:2, 3; Hebrews 1:2; Job 26:13; Romans 1:20; Colossians 1:16; Genesis 1:31)

2)   After God had made all other creatures, he created man, male and female, with reasonable and immortal souls, rendering them fit unto that life to God for which they were created; being made after the image of God, in knowledge, righteousness, and true holiness; having the law of God written in their hearts, and power to fulfil it, and yet under a possibility of transgressing, being left to the liberty of their own will, which was subject to change.

(Genesis 1:27; Genesis 2:7; Ecclesiastes 7:29; Genesis 1:26; Romans 2:14, 15; Genesis 3:6)

3)   Besides the law written in their hearts, they received a command not to eat of the tree of knowledge of good and evil, which whilst they kept, they were happy in their communion with God, and had dominion over the creatures. (Genesis 2:17; Genesis 1:26, 28)

Chapter 5:Of Divine Providence

1)   God the good Creator of all things, in his infinite power and wisdom doth uphold, direct, dispose, and govern all creatures and things, from the greatest even to the least, by his most wise and holy providence, to the end for the which they were created, according unto his infallible foreknowledge, and the free and immutable counsel of his own will; to the praise of the glory of his wisdom, power, justice, infinite goodness, and mercy.
(Hebrews 1:3; Job 38:11; Isaiah 46:10, 11; Psalms 135:6; Matthew 10:29-31; Ephesians 1:11)

2)   Although in relation to the foreknowledge and decree of God, the first cause, all things come to pass immutably and infallibly; so that there is not anything befalls any by chance, or without his providence; yet by the same providence he ordereth them to fall out according to the nature of second causes, either necessarily, freely, or contingently.

(Acts 2:23; Proverbs 16:33; Genesis 8:22)

3)   God, in his ordinary providence maketh use of means, yet is free to work without, above, and against them at his pleasure.

(Acts 27:31, 44; Isaiah 55:10, 11; Hosea 1:7; Romans 4:19-21; Daniel 3:27)

4)   The almighty power, unsearchable wisdom, and infinite goodness of God, so far manifest themselves in his providence, that his determinate counsel extendeth itself

even to the first fall, and all other sinful actions both of angels and men; and that not by a bare permission, which also he most wisely and powerfully boundeth, and otherwise ordereth and governeth, in a manifold dispensation to his most holy ends; yet so, as the sinfulness of their acts proceedeth only from the creatures, and not from God, who, being most holy and righteous, neither is nor can be the author or approver of sin.

(Romans 11:32-34; 2 Samuel 24:1, 1 Chronicles 21:1; 2 Kings 19:28; Psalms 76;10; Genesis 1:20; Isaiah 10:6, 7, 12; Psalms 1:21; 1 John 2:16)

5)   The most wise, righteous, and gracious God doth oftentimes leave for a season his own children to manifold temptations and the corruptions of their own hearts, to chastise them for their former sins, or to discover unto them the hidden strength of corruption and deceitfulness of their hearts, that they may be humbled; and to raise them to a more close and constant dependence for their support upon himself; and to make them more watchful against all future occasions of sin, and for other just and holy ends. So that whatsoever befalls any of his elect is by his appointment, for his glory, and their good.
(2 Chronicles 32:25, 26, 31; 2 Corinthians 12:7-9; Romans 8:28)

6)   As for those wicked and ungodly men whom God, as the righteous judge, for former sin doth blind and harden; from them he not only withholdeth his grace, whereby they might have been enlightened in their understanding, and wrought upon their hearts; but sometimes also withdraweth the gifts which they had, and exposeth them to such objects as their corruption makes occasion of sin; and withal, gives

them over to their own lusts, the temptations of the world, and the power of Satan, whereby it comes to pass that they harden themselves, under those means which God useth for the softening of others.

(Romans 1:24-26, 28; Romans 11:7, 8; Deuteronomy 29:4; Matthew 13:12; Deuteronomy 2:30; 2 Kings 8:12, 13; Psalms 81:11, 12; 2 Thessalonians 2:10-12; Exodus 8:15, 32; Isaiah 6:9, 10; 1 Peter 2:7, 8)

7)   As the providence of God doth in general reach to all creatures, so after a more special manner it taketh care of his church, and disposeth of all things to the good thereof.

(1 Timothy 4:10; Amos 9:8, 9; Isaiah 43:3-5)

Chapter 6: Of the Fall of Man, Of Sin, And of the Punishment.

1)   Although God created man upright and perfect, and gave him a righteous law, which had been unto life had he kept it, and threatened death upon the breach thereof, yet he did not long abide in this honour; Satan using the subtlety of the serpent to subdue Eve, then by her seducing Adam, who, without any compulsion, did willfully transgress the law of their creation, and the command given unto them, in eating the forbidden fruit, which God was pleased, according to his wise and holy counsel to permit, having purposed to order it to his own glory.

(Genesis 2:16, 17; Genesis 3:12,13; 2 Corinthians 11:3)

2)   Our first parents, by this sin, fell from their original righteousness and communion with God, and we in them whereby death came upon all: all becoming dead in sin, and wholly defiled in all the faculties and parts of soul and body.

(Romans 3:23; Romans 5:12, etc; Titus 1:15; Genesis 6:5; Jeremiah 17:9; Romans 3:10-19)

3)   They being the root, and by God's appointment, standing in the room and stead of all mankind, the guilt of the sin was imputed, and corrupted nature conveyed, to all their posterity descending from them by ordinary generation, being now conceived in sin, and by nature children of wrath, the servants of sin, the subjects of death, and all other

miseries, spiritual, temporal, and eternal, unless the Lord Jesus set them free.

(Romans 5:12-19; 1 Corinthians 15:21, 22, 45, 49; Psalms 51:5; Job 14:4; Ephesians 2:3; Romans 6:20 Romans 5:12; Hebrews 2:14, 15; 1 Thessalonians 1:10)

4)   From this original corruption, whereby we are utterly indisposed, disabled, and made opposite to all good, and wholly inclined to all evil, do proceed all actual transgressions.

(Romans 8:7; Colossians 1:21; James 1:14, 15; Matthew 15:19)

5)   The corruption of nature, during this life, doth remain in those that are regenerated; and although it be through Christ pardoned and mortified, yet both itself, and the first motions thereof, are truly and properly sin.

(Romans 7:18,23; Ecclesiastes 7:20; 1 John 1:8; Romans 7:23-25; Galatians 5:17)

Chapter 7:Of God's Covenant

1) The distance between God and the creature is so great, that although reasonable creatures do owe obedience to him as their creator, yet they could never have attained the reward of life but by some voluntary condescension on God's part, which he hath been pleased to express by way of covenant.

(Luke 17:10; Job 35:7,8)

2) Moreover, man having brought himself under the curse of the law by his fall, it pleased the Lord to make a covenant of grace, wherein he freely offereth unto sinners life and salvation by Jesus Christ, requiring of them faith in him, that they may be saved; and promising to give unto all those that are ordained unto eternal life, his Holy
Spirit, to make them willing and able to believe.

(Genesis 2:17; Galatians 3:10; Romans 3:20, 21; Romans 8:3; Mark 16:15, 16; John 3:16; Ezekiel 36:26, 27; John 6:44, 45; Psalms 110:3)

3) This covenant is revealed in the gospel; first of all to Adam in the promise of salvation by the seed of the woman, and afterwards by farther steps, until the full discovery thereof was completed in the New Testament; and it is founded in that eternal covenant transaction that was between the Father and the Son about the redemption of the elect; and it is alone by the grace of this covenant that all the posterity of fallen Adam that ever were saved did obtain life and blessed immortality, man being now utterly incapable of

acceptance with God upon those terms on which Adam stood in his state of innocency.

(Genesis 3:15; Hebrews 1:1; 2 Timothy 1:9; Titus 1:2; Hebrews 11;6, 13; Romans 4:1, 2; Acts 4:12; John 8:56)

Chapter 8: Of Christ the Mediator

1) It pleased God, in His eternal purpose, to choose and ordain the Lord Jesus, his only begotten Son, according to the covenant made between them both, to be the mediator between God and man; the prophet, priest, and king; head and saviour of the church, the heir of all things, and judge of the world; unto whom he did from all eternity give a people to be his seed and to be by him in time redeemed, called, justified, sanctified, and glorified.

(Isaiah 42:1; 1 Peter 1:19, 20; Acts 3:22; Hebrews 5:5, 6; Psalms 2:6; Luke 1:33; Ephesians 1:22, 23; Hebrews 1:2; Acts 17:31; Isaiah 53:10; John 17:6; Romans 8:30)

2) The Son of God, the second person in the Holy Trinity, being very and eternal God, the brightness of the Father's glory, of one substance and equal with him who made the world, who upholdeth and governeth all things he hath made, did, when the fullness of time was come, take upon him man's nature, with all the essential properties and common infirmities thereof, yet without sin; being conceived by the Holy Spirit in the womb of the Virgin Mary, the Holy Spirit coming down upon her: and the power of the Most High overshadowing her; and so was made of a woman of the tribe of Judah, of the seed of Abraham and David according to the Scriptures; so that two whole, perfect, and distinct natures were inseparably joined together in one person, without conversion, composition, or confusion; which person is very God and very man, yet one Christ, the only mediator between God and man.

(John 1:14; Galatians 4;4; Romans 8:3; Hebrews 2:14, 16, 17; Hebrews 4:15; Matthew 1:22, 23; Luke 1:27, 31, 35; Romans 9:5; 1 Timothy 2:5)

3_ The Lord Jesus, in his human nature thus united to the divine, in the person of the Son, was sanctified and anointed with the Holy Spirit above measure, having in Him all the treasures of wisdom and knowledge; in whom it pleased the Father that all fullness should dwell, to the end that being holy, harmless, undefiled, and full of grace and truth, he might be throughly furnished to execute the office of mediator and surety; which office he took not upon himself, but was thereunto called by his Father; who also put all power and judgement in his hand, and gave him commandment to execute the same.

(Psalms 45:7; Acts 10:38; John 3:34; Colossians 2:3; Colossians 1:19; Hebrews 7:26; John 1:14; Hebrews 7:22; Hebrews 5:5; John 5:22, 27; Matthew 28:18; Acts 2:36)

4) This office the Lord Jesus did most willingly undertake, which that he might discharge he was made under the law, and did perfectly fulfil it, and underwent the punishment due to us, which we should have borne and suffered, being made sin and a curse for us; enduring most grievous sorrows in his soul, and most painful sufferings in his body; was crucified, and died, and remained in the state of the dead, yet saw no corruption: on the third day he arose from the dead with the same body in which he suffered, with which he also ascended into heaven, and there sitteth at the right hand of his Father making intercession, and shall return to judge men and angels at the end of the world.

(Psalms 40:7, 8; Hebrews 10:5-10; John 10:18; Gal 4:4; Matthew 3:15; Galatians 3:13; Isaiah 53:6; 1 Peter 3:18; 2

Corinthians 5:21; Matthew 26:37, 38; Luke 22:44; Matthew 27:46; Acts 13:37; 1 Corinthians 15:3, 4; John 20:25, 27; Mark 16:19; Acts 1:9-11; Romans 8:34; Hebrews 9:24; Acts 10:42; Romans 14:9, 10; Acts 1:11; 2 Peter 2:4)

5)   The Lord Jesus, by his perfect obedience and sacrifice of himself, which he through the eternal Spirit once offered up unto God, hath fully satisfied the justice of God, procured reconciliation, and purchased an everlasting inheritance in the kingdom of heaven, for all those whom the Father hath given unto Him.

(Hebrews 9:14; Hebrews 10:14; Romans 3:25, 26; John 17:2; Hebrews 9:15)

6)   Although the price of redemption was not actually paid by Christ till after his incarnation, yet the virtue, efficacy, and benefit thereof were communicated to the elect in all ages, successively from the beginning of the world, in and by those promises, types, and sacrifices wherein he was revealed, and signified to be the seed which should bruise the serpent's head; and the Lamb slain from the foundation of the world, being the same yesterday, and to-day and for ever.

(1 Corinthians 4:10; Hebrews 4:2; 1 Peter 1:10, 11; Revelation 13:8; Hebrews 13:8)

7)   Christ, in the work of mediation, acteth according to both natures, by each nature doing that which is proper to itself; yet by reason of the unity of the person, that which is proper to one nature is sometimes in Scripture, attributed to the person denominated by the other nature.

(John 3:13; Acts 20:28)

8)   To all those for whom Christ hath obtained eternal redemption, he doth certainly and effectually apply and communicate the same, making intercession for them; uniting them to himself by his Spirit, revealing unto them, in and by his Word, the mystery of salvation, persuading them to believe and obey, governing their hearts by his Word and Spirit, and overcoming all their enemies by his almighty power and wisdom, in such manner and ways as are most consonant to his wonderful and unsearchable dispensation; and all of free and absolute grace, without any condition foreseen in them to procure it.
(John 6:37; John 10:15, 16; John 17:9; Romans 5:10; John 17:6; Ephesians 1:9; 1 John 5:20; Romans 8:9, 14; Psalms 110:1; 1 Corinthians 15:25, 26; John 3:8; Ephesians 1:8)

9)   This office of mediator between God and man is proper only to Christ, who is the prophet, priest, and king of the church of God; and may not be either in whole, or any part thereof, transferred from him to any other.

(1 Timothy 2:5)

10)   This number and order of offices is necessary; for in respect of our ignorance, we stand in need of his prophetical office; and in respect of our alienation from God, and imperfection of the best of our services, we need his priestly office to reconcile us and present us acceptable unto God; and in respect to our averseness and utter inability to return to God, and for our rescue and security from our spiritual adversaries, we need his kingly office to convince, subdue,

draw, uphold, deliver, and preserve us to his heavenly kingdom.
(John 1:18; Colossians 1:21; Galatians 5:17; John 16:8; Psalms 110:3; Luke 1:74, 75)

Chapter 9: Of Free Will

1) God hath endued the will of man with that natural liberty and power of acting upon choice, that it is neither forced, nor by any necessity of nature determined to do good or evil.

(Matthew 17:12; James 1:14; Deuteronomy 30:19)

2) Man, in his state of innocency, had freedom and power to will and to do that which was good and well-pleasing to God, but yet was unstable, so that he might fall from it.

(Ecclesiastes 7:29; Genesis 3:6)

3) Man, by his fall into a state of sin, hath wholly lost all ability of will to any spiritual good accompanying salvation; so as a natural man, being altogether averse from that good, and dead in sin, is not able by his own strength to convert himself, or to prepare himself thereunto.
(Romans 5:6; Romans 8:7; Ephesians 2:1, 5; Titus 3:3-5; John 6:44)

4) When God converts a sinner, and translates him into the state of grace, he freeth him from his natural bondage under sin, and by his grace alone enables him freely to will and to do that which is spiritually good; yet so as that by reason of his remaining corruptions, he doth not perfectly, nor only will, that which is good, but doth also will that which is evil.

(Colossians 1:13; John 8:36; Philippians 2:13; Romans 7:15, 18, 19, 21, 23)

5)   This will of man is made perfectly and immutably free to good alone in the state of glory only.
(Ephesians 4:13)

Chapter 10: Of Effectual Calling

1)   Those whom God hath predestinated unto life, he is pleased in his appointed, and accepted time, effectually to call, by his Word and Spirit, out of that state of sin and death in which they are by nature, to grace and salvation by Jesus Christ; enlightening their minds spiritually and savingly to understand the things of God; taking away their heart of stone, and giving unto them a heart of flesh; renewing their wills, and by his almighty power determining them to that which is good, and effectually drawing them to Jesus Christ; yet so as they come most freely, being made willing by his grace.

(Romans 8:30; Romans 11:7; Ephesians 1:10, 11; 2 Thessalonians 2:13, 14; Ephesians 2:1-6; Acts 26:18; Ephesians 1:17, 18; Ezekiel 36:26; Deuteronomy 30:6; Ezekiel 36:27; Ephesians 1:19; Psalm 110:3; Song of Solomon 1:4)

2)   This effectual call is of God's free and special grace alone, not from anything at all foreseen in man, nor from any power or agency in the creature, being wholly passive therein, being dead in sins and trespasses, until being quickened and renewed by the Holy Spirit; he is thereby enabled to answer this call, and to embrace the grace offered and conveyed in it, and that by no less power than that which raised up Christ from the dead.

(2 Timothy 1:9; Ephesians 2:8; 1 Corinthians 2:14; Ephesians 2:5; John 5:25; Ephesians 1:19, 20)

3)   Elect infants dying in infancy are regenerated and saved by Christ through the Spirit; who worketh when, and where, and how he pleases; so also are all elect persons, who are incapable of being outwardly called by the ministry of the Word.

(John 3:3, 5, 6; John 3:8)

4)   Others not elected, although they may be called by the ministry of the Word, and may have some common operations of the Spirit, yet not being effectually drawn by the Father, they neither will nor can truly come to Christ, and therefore cannot be saved: much less can men that receive not the Christian religion be saved; be they never so diligent to frame their lives according to the light of nature and the law of that religion they do profess.

(Matthew 22:14; Matthew 13:20, 21; Hebrews 6:4, 5; John 6:44, 45, 65; 1 John 2:24, 25; Acts 4:12; John 4:22; John 17:3)

Chapter 11: Of Justification

1)   Those whom God effectually calleth, he also freely justifieth, not by infusing righteousness into them, but by pardoning their sins, and by accounting and accepting their persons as righteous; not for anything wrought in them, or done by them, but for Christ's sake alone; not by imputing faith itself, the act of believing, or any other evangelical obedience to them, as their righteousness; but by imputing Christ's active obedience unto the whole law, and passive obedience in his death for their whole and sole righteousness by faith, which faith they have not of themselves; it is the gift of God.

(Romans 3:24; Romans 8:30; Romans 4:5-8; Ephesians 1:7; 1 Corinthians 1:30, 31; Romans 5:17-19; Philippians 3:8, 9; Ephesians 2:8-10; John 1:12; Romans 5:17)

2)   Faith thus receiving and resting on Christ and his righteousness, is the alone instrument of justification; yet it is not alone in the person justified, but is ever accompanied with all other saving graces, and is no dead faith, but worketh by love.

(Romans 3:28; Galatians 5:6; James 2:17, 22, 26)

3)   Christ, by his obedience and death, did fully discharge the debt of all those that are justified; and did, by the sacrifice of himself in the blood of his cross, undergoing in their stead the penalty due unto them, make a proper, real, and full satisfaction to God's justice in their behalf; yet,

inasmuch as he was given by the Father for them, and his obedience and satisfaction accepted in their stead, and both freely, not for anything in them, their justification is only of free grace, that both the exact justice and rich grace of God might be glorified in the justification of sinners.

(Hebrews 10:14; 1 Peter 1:18, 19; Isaiah 53:5, 6; Romans 8:32; 2 Corinthians 5:21; Romans 3:26; Ephesians 1:6,7; Ephesians 2:7)

4)   God did from all eternity decree to justify all the elect, and Christ did in the fullness of time die for their sins, and rise again for their justification; nevertheless, they are not justified personally, until the Holy Spirit doth in time due actually apply Christ unto them.
(Galatians 3:8; 1 Peter 1:2; 1 Timothy 2:6; Romans 4:25; Colossians 1:21,22; Titus 3:4-7)

5)   God doth continue to forgive the sins of those that are justified, and although they can never fall from the state of justification, yet they may, by their sins, fall under God's fatherly displeasure; and in that condition they have not usually the light of his countenance restored unto them, until they humble themselves, confess their sins, beg pardon, and renew their faith and repentance.

(Matthew 6:12; 1 John 1:7, 9; John 10:28; Psalms 89:31-33; Psalms 32:5; Psalms 51; Matthew 26:75)

6)   The justification of believers under the Old Testament was, in all these respects, one and the same with the justification of believers under the New Testament.

(Galatians 3:9; Romans 4:22-24)

Chapter 12: Of Adoption

1)   All those that are justified, God vouchsafed, in and for the sake of his only Son Jesus Christ, to make partakers of the grace of adoption, by which they are taken into the number, and enjoy the liberties and privileges of the children of God, have his name put upon them, receive the spirit of adoption, have access to the throne of grace with boldness, are enabled to cry Abba, Father, are pitied, protected, provided for, and chastened by him as by a Father, yet never cast off, but sealed to the day of redemption, and inherit the promises as heirs of everlasting salvation.

(Ephesians 1:5; Galatians 4:4, 5; John 1:12; Romans 8:17; 2 Corinthians 6:18; Revelation 3:12; Romans 8:15; Galatians 4:6; Ephesians 2:18; Psalms 103:13; Proverbs 14:26; 1 Peter 5:7; Hebrews 12:6; Isaiah 54:8, 9; Lamentations 3:31; Ephesians 4:30; Hebrews 1:14; Hebrews 6:12)

Chapter 13: Of Sanctification

1)   They who are united to Christ, effectually called, and regenerated, having a new heart and a new spirit created in them through the virtue of Christ's death and resurrection, are also farther sanctified, really and personally, through the same virtue, by His Word and Spirit dwelling in them; the dominion of the whole body of sin is destroyed, and the several lusts thereof are more and more weakened and mortified, and they more and more quickened and strengthened in all saving graces, to the practice of all true holiness, without which no man shall see the Lord.

(Acts 20:32; Romans 6:5, 6; John 17:17; Ephesians 3:16-19; 1 Thessalonians 5:21-23; Romans 6:14; Galatians 5:24; Colossians 1:11; 2 Corinthians 7:1; Hebrews 12:14)

2)   This sanctification is throughout the whole man, yet imperfect in this life; there abideth still some remnants of corruption in every part, whence ariseth a continual and irreconcilable war; the flesh lusting against the Spirit, and the Spirit against the flesh.

(1 Thessalonians 5:23; Romans 7:18, 23; Galatians 5:17; 1 Peter 2:11)

3)   In which war, although the remaining corruption for a time may much prevail, yet through the continual supply of strength from the sanctifying Spirit of Christ, the regenerate part doth overcome; and so the saints grow in grace, perfecting holiness in the fear of God, pressing after an heavenly life, in evangelical obedience to all the commands

which Christ as Head and King, in His Word hath prescribed them.

(Romans 7:23; Romans 6:14; Ephesians 4:15, 16; 2 Corinthians 3:18; 2 Corinthians 7:1)

Chapter 14: Of Saving Faith

1)   The grace of faith, whereby the elect are enabled to believe to the saving of their souls, is the work of the Spirit of Christ in their hearts, and is ordinarily wrought by the ministry of the Word; by which also, and by the administration of baptism and the Lord's supper, prayer, and other means appointed of God, it is increased and strengthened.
(2 Corinthians 4:13; Ephesians 2:8; Romans 10:14, 17; Luke 17:5; 1 Peter 2:2; Acts 20:32)

2)By this faith a Christian believeth to be true whatsoever is revealed in the Word for the authority of God himself, and also apprehendeth an excellency therein above all other writings and all things in the world, as it bears forth the glory of God in his attributes, the excellency of Christ in his nature and offices, and the power and fullness of the Holy Spirit in his workings and operations: and so is enabled to cast his soul upon the truth thus believed; and also acteth differently upon that which each particular passage thereof containeth; yielding obedience to the commands, trembling at the threatenings, and embracing the promises of God for this life and that which is to come; but the principal acts of saving faith have immediate relation to Christ, accepting, receiving, and resting upon him alone for justification, sanctification, and eternal life, by virtue of the covenant of grace.

(Acts 24:14; Psalms 27:7-10; Psalms 119:72; 2 Timothy 1:12; John 14:14; Isaiah 66:2; Hebrews 11:13; John 1:12; Acts 16:31; Galatians 2:20; Acts 15:11)

3) This faith, although it be different in degrees, and may be weak or strong, yet it is in the least degree of it different in the kind or nature of it, as is all other saving grace, from the faith and common grace of temporary believers; and therefore, though it may be many times assailed and weakened, yet it gets the victory, growing up in many to the attainment of a full assurance through Christ, who is both the author and finisher of our faith.

(Hebrews 5:13, 14; Matthew 6:30; Romans 4:19, 20; 2 Peter 1:1; Ephesians 6:16; 1 John 5:4, 5; Hebrews 6:11, 12; Colossians 2:2; Hebrews 12:2)

Chapter 15: Of Repentance Unto Life and Salvation

1) Such of the elect as are converted at riper years, having sometime lived in the state of nature, and therein served divers lusts and pleasures, God in their effectual calling giveth them repentance unto life. (Titus 3:2-5)

2) Whereas there is none that doth good and sinneth not, and the best of men may, through the power and deceitfulness of their corruption dwelling in them, with the prevalency of temptation, fall into great sins and provocations; God hath, in the covenant of grace, mercifully provided that believers so sinning and falling be renewed through repentance unto salvation.

(Ecclesiastes 7:20; Luke 22:31, 32)

3) This saving repentance is an evangelical grace, whereby a person, being by the Holy Spirit made sensible of the manifold evils of his sin, doth, by faith in Christ, humble himself for it with godly sorrow, detestation of it, and self-abhorrency, praying for pardon and strength of grace, with a purpose and endeavour, by supplies of the Spirit, to walk before God unto all well-pleasing in all things.

(Zechariah 12:10; Acts 11:18; Ezekiel 36:31; 2 Corinthians 7:11; Psalms 119:6; Psalms 119:128)

4) As repentance is to be continued through the whole course of our lives, upon the account of the body of death,

and the motions thereof, so it is every man's duty to repent of his particular known sins particularly.

(Luke 19:8; 1 Timothy 1:13, 15)

5)   Such is the provision which God hath made through Christ in the covenant of grace for the preservation of believers unto salvation; that although there is no sin so small but it deserves damnation; yet there is no sin so great that it shall bring damnation on them that repent; which makes the constant preaching of repentance necessary.

(Romans 6:23; Isaiah 1:16-18 Isaiah 55:7)

Chapter 16: Of Good Works

1)   Good works are only such as God hath commanded in his Holy Word, and not such as without the warrant thereof are devised by men out of blind zeal, or upon any pretence of good intentions.

(Micah 6:8; Hebrews 13:21; Matthew 15:9; Isaiah 29:13)

2)   These good works, done in obedience to God's commandments, are the fruits and evidences of a true and lively faith; and by them believers manifest their thankfulness, strengthen their assurance, edify their brethren, adorn the profession of the gospel, stop the mouths of the adversaries, and glorify God, whose workmanship they are, created in Christ Jesus thereunto, that having their fruit unto holiness they may have the end eternal life.

(James 2:18, 22; Psalms 116:12, 13; 1 John 2:3, 5; 2 Peter 1:5-11; Matthew 5:16; 1 Timothy 6:1; 1 Peter 2:15; Philippians 1:11; Ephesians 2:10; Romans 6:22)

3)   Their ability to do good works is not at all of themselves, but wholly from the Spirit of Christ; and that they may be enabled thereunto, besides the graces they have already received, there is necessary an actual influence of the same Holy Spirit, to work in them to will and to do of his good pleasure; yet they are not hereupon to grow negligent, as if they were not bound to perform any duty, unless upon a special motion of the Spirit, but they ought to be diligent in stirring up the grace of God that is in them.

(John 15:4, 5; 2 Corinthians 3:5; Philippians 2:13; Philippians 2:12; Hebrews 6:11, 12; Isaiah 64:7)

4) They who in their obedience attain to the greatest height which is possible in this life, are so far from being able to supererogate, and to do more than God requires, as that they fall short of much which in duty they are bound to do.

(Job 9:2, 3; Galatians 5:17; Luke 17:10)

5) We cannot by our best works merit pardon of sin or eternal life at the hand of God, by reason of the great disproportion that is between them and the glory to come, and the infinite distance that is between us and God, whom by them we can neither profit nor satisfy for the debt of our former sins; but when we have done all we can, we have done but our duty, and are unprofitable servants; and because as they are good they proceed from his Spirit, and as they are wrought by us they are defiled and mixed with so much weakness and imperfection, that they cannot endure the severity of God's punishment.

(Romans 3:20; Ephesians 2:8, 9; Romans 4:6; Galatians 5:22, 23; Isaiah 64:6; Psalms 143:2)

6) Yet notwithstanding the persons of believers being accepted through Christ, their good works also are accepted in him; not as though they were in this life wholly unblameable and unreprovable in God's sight, but that he, looking upon them in his Son, is pleased to accept and reward that which is sincere, although accompanied with many weaknesses and imperfections.

(Ephesians 1:6; 1 Peter 2:5; Matthew 25:21, 23; Hebrews 6:10)

7)   Works done by unregenerate men, although for the matter of them they may be things which God commands, and of good use both to themselves and others; yet because they proceed not from a heart purified by faith, nor are done in a right manner according to the word, nor to a right end, the glory of God, they are therefore sinful, and cannot please God, nor make a man meet to receive grace from God, and yet their neglect of them is more sinful and displeasing to God.

(2 Kings 10:30; 1 Kings 21:27, 29; Genesis 4:5; Hebrews 11:4, 6; 1 Corinthians 13:1; Matthew 6:2, 5; Amos 5:21, 22; Romans 9:16; Titus 3:5; Job 21:14, 15; Matthew 25:41-43)

Chapter 17: Of The Perseverance of the Saints

1)   Those whom God hath accepted in the beloved, effectually called and sanctified by his Spirit, and given the precious faith of his elect unto, can neither totally nor finally fall from the state of grace, but shall certainly persevere therein to the end, and be eternally saved, seeing the gifts and callings of God are without repentance, whence he still begets and nourisheth in them faith, repentance, love, joy, hope, and all the graces of the Spirit unto immortality; and though many storms and floods arise and beat against them, yet they shall never be able to take them off that foundation and rock which by faith they are fastened upon; notwithstanding, through unbelief and the temptations of Satan, the sensible sight of the light and love of God may for a time be clouded and obscured from them, yet he is still the same, and they shall be sure to be kept by the power of God unto salvation, where they shall enjoy their purchased possession, they being engraven upon the palm of his hands, and their names having been written in the book of life from all eternity.

(John 10:28, 29; Philippians 1:6; 2 Timothy 2:19; 1 John 2:19; Psalms 89:31, 32; 1 Corinthians 11:32; Malachi 3:6)

2)   This perseverance of the saints depends not upon their own free will, but upon the immutability of the decree of election, flowing from the free and unchangeable love of God the Father, upon the efficacy of the merit and intercession of Jesus Christ and union with him, the oath of

God, the abiding of his Spirit, and the seed of God within them, and the nature of the covenant of grace; from all which ariseth also the certainty and infallibility thereof.

(Romans 8:30 Romans 9:11, 16; Romans 5:9, 10; John 14:19; Hebrews 6:17, 18; 1 John 3:9; Jeremiah 32:40)

3._____ And though they may, through the temptation of Satan and of the world, the prevalency of corruption remaining in them, and the neglect of means of their preservation, fall into grievous sins, and for a time continue therein, whereby they incur God's displeasure and grieve his Holy Spirit, come to have their graces and comforts impaired, have their hearts hardened, and their consciences wounded, hurt and scandalize others, and bring temporal judgments upon themselves, yet shall they renew their repentance and be preserved through faith in Christ Jesus to the end.

(Matthew 26:70, 72, 74; Isaiah 64:5, 9; Ephesians 4:30; Psalms 51:10, 12; Psalms 32:3, 4; 2 Samuel 12:14; Luke 22:32, 61, 62)

Chapter 18: Of the Assurance of Grace and Salvation

1)   Although temporary believers, and other unregenerate men, may vainly deceive themselves with false hopes and carnal presumptions of being in the favour of God and state of salvation, which hope of theirs shall perish; yet such as truly believe in the Lord Jesus, and love him in sincerity, endeavouring to walk in all good conscience before him, may in this life be certainly assured that they are in the state of grace, and may rejoice in the hope of the glory of God, which hope shall never make them ashamed.

(Job 8:13, 14; Matthew 7:22, 23; 1 John 2:3; 1 John 3:14, 18, 19, 21, 24; 1 John 5:13; Romans 5:2, 5)

2)   This certainty is not a bare conjectural and probable persuasion grounded upon a fallible hope, but an infallible assurance of faith founded on the blood and righteousness of Christ revealed in the Gospel; and also upon the inward evidence of those graces of the Spirit unto which promises are made, and on the testimony of the Spirit of adoption, witnessing with our spirits that we are the children of God; and, as a fruit thereof, keeping the heart both humble and holy.

(Hebrews 6:11, 19; Hebrews 6:17, 18; 2 Peter 1:4, 5, 10, 11; Romans 8:15, 16; 1 John 3:1-3)

3)   This infallible assurance doth not so belong to the essence of faith, but that a true believer may wait long, and

conflict with many difficulties before he be partaker of it; yet being enabled by the Spirit to know the things which are freely given him of God, he may, without extraordinary revelation, in the right use of means, attain thereunto: and therefore it is the duty of every one to give all diligence to make his calling and election sure, that thereby his heart may be enlarged in peace and joy in the Holy Spirit, in love and thankfulness to God, and in strength and cheerfulness in the duties of obedience, the proper fruits of this assurance; -so far is it from inclining men to looseness.

(Isaiah 50:10; Psalms 88; Psalms 77:1-12; 1 John 4:13; Hebrews 6:11, 12; Romans 5:1, 2, 5; Romans 14:17; Psalms 119:32; Romans 6:1,2; Titus 2:11, 12, 14)

4)   True believers may have the assurance of their salvation divers ways shaken, diminished, and intermitted; as by negligence in preserving of it, by falling into some special sin which woundeth the conscience and grieveth the Spirit; by some sudden or vehement temptation, by God's withdrawing the light of his countenance, and suffering even such as fear him to walk in darkness and to have no light, yet are they never destitute of the seed of God and life of faith, that love of Christ and the brethren, that sincerity of heart and conscience of duty out of which, by the operation of the Spirit, this assurance may in due time be revived, and by the which, in the meantime, they are
preserved from utter despair.

(Psalms 51:8, 12, 14; Psalms 116:11; Psalms 77:7, 8; Psalms 31:22; Psalms 30:7; 1 John 3:9; Luke 22:32; Psalms 42:5, 11; Lamentations 3:26-31)

Chapter 19: Of the Law of God

1)   God gave to Adam a law of universal obedience written in his heart, and a particular precept of not eating the fruit of the tree of knowledge of good and evil; by which he bound him and all his posterity to personal, entire, exact, and perpetual obedience; promised life upon the fulfilling, and threatened death upon the breach of it, and endued him with power and ability to keep it.

(Genesis 1:27; Ecclesiastes 7:29; Romans 10:5; Galatians 3:10, 12)

2)   The same law that was first written in the heart of man continued to be a perfect rule of righteousness after the fall, and was delivered by God upon Mount Sinai, in ten commandments, and written in two tables, the four first containing our duty towards God, and the other six, our duty to man.

(Romans 2:14, 15; Deuteronomy 10:4)

3)   Besides this law, commonly called moral, God was pleased to give to the people of Israel ceremonial laws, containing several typical ordinances, partly of worship, prefiguring Christ, his graces, actions, sufferings, and benefits; and partly holding forth divers instructions of moral duties, all which ceremonial laws being appointed only to the time of reformation, are, by Jesus Christ the true Messiah and only law-giver, who was furnished with power from the Father for that end abrogated and taken away.

(Hebrews 10:1; Colossians 2:17; 1 Corinthians 5:7;
Colossians 2:14, 16, 17; Ephesians 2:14, 16)

4) To them also he gave sundry judicial laws, which expired
together with the state of that people, not obliging any now
by virtue of that institution; their general equity only being of
moral use.

(1 Corinthians 9:8-10)

5) The moral law doth for ever bind all, as well justified
persons as others, to the obedience thereof, and that not
only in regard of the matter contained in it, but also in
respect of the authority of God the Creator, who gave it;
neither doth Christ in the Gospel any way dissolve, but much
strengthen this obligation.

(Romans 13:8-10; James 2:8, 10-12; James 2:10, 11;
Matthew 5:17-19; Romans 3:31)

6.) Although true believers be not under the law as a
covenant of works, to be thereby justified or condemned, yet
it is of great use to them as well as to others, in that as a rule
of life, informing them of the will of God and their duty, it
directs and binds them to walk accordingly; discovering also
the sinful pollutions of their natures, hearts, and lives, so as
examining themselves thereby, they may come to further
conviction of, humiliation for, and hatred against, sin;
together with a clearer sight of the need they have of Christ
and the perfection of his obedience; it is likewise of use to
the regenerate to restrain their corruptions, in that it forbids
sin; and the threatenings of it serve to shew what even their
sins deserve, and what afflictions in this life they may expect
for them, although freed from the curse and unallayed rigour
thereof.

The promises of it likewise shew them God's approbation of obedience, and what blessings they may expect upon the performance thereof, though not as due to them by the law as a covenant of works; so as man's doing good and refraining from evil, because the law encourageth to the one and deterreth from the other, is no evidence of his being under the law and not under grace.

(Romans 6:14; Galatians 2:16; Romans 8:1; Romans 10:4; Romans 3:20; Romans 6:12-14; 1 Peter 3:8-13)

7)   Neither are the aforementioned uses of the law contrary to the grace of the Gospel, but do sweetly comply with it, the Spirit of Christ subduing and enabling the will of man to do that freely and cheerfully which the will of God, revealed in the law, requireth to be done.

(Galatians 3:21; Ezekiel 36:27)

Chapter 20: Of the Gospel, and of the Extent of the Grace

1)   The covenant of works being broken by sin, and made unprofitable unto life, God was pleased to give forth the promise of Christ, the seed of the woman, as the means of calling the elect, and begetting in them faith and repentance; in this promise the gospel, as to the substance of it, was revealed, and [is] therein effectual for the conversion and salvation of sinners.

(Genesis 3:15; Revelation 13:8)

2)   This promise of Christ, and salvation by him, is revealed only by the Word of God; neither do the works of creation or providence, with the light of nature, make discovery of Christ, or of grace by him, so much as in a general or obscure way; much less that men destitute of the revelation of Him by the promise or gospel, should be enabled thereby to attain saving faith or repentance.

(Romans 1:17; Romans 10:14,15,17; Proverbs 29:18; Isaiah 25:7; Isaiah 60:2, 3)

3)   The revelation of the gospel unto sinners, made in divers times and by sundry parts, with the addition of promises and precepts for the obedience required therein, as to the nations and persons to whom it is granted, is merely of the sovereign will and good pleasure of God; not being annexed by virtue of any promise to the due improvement of men's natural abilities, by virtue of common light received without it,

which none ever did make, or can do so; and therefore in all ages, the preaching of the gospel has been granted unto persons and nations, as to the extent or straitening of it, in great variety, according to the counsel of the will of God.

(Psalms 147:20; Acts 16:7; Romans 1:18-32)

4)   Although the gospel be the only outward means of revealing Christ and saving grace, and is, as such, abundantly sufficient thereunto; yet that men who are dead in trespasses may be born again, quickened or regenerated, there is moreover necessary an effectual insuperable work of the Holy Spirit upon the whole soul, for the producing in them a new spiritual life; without which no other means will effect their conversion unto God.
(Psalms 110:3; 1 Corinthians 2:14; Ephesians 1:19, 20; John 6:44; 2 Corinthians 4:4, 6)

Chapter 21: Of Christian Liberty and Liberty of **Conscience**

1)   The liberty which Christ hath purchased for believers under the gospel, consists in their freedom from the guilt of sin, the condemning wrath of God, the rigour and curse of the law, and in their being delivered from this present evil world, bondage to Satan, and dominion of sin, from the evil of afflictions, the fear and sting of death, the victory of the grave, and ever- lasting damnation: as also in their free access to God, and their yielding obedience unto Him, not out of slavish fear, but a child-like love and willing mind. All which were common also to believers under the law for the substance of them; but under the New Testament the liberty of Christians is further enlarged, in their freedom from the yoke of a ceremonial law, to which the Jewish church was subjected, and in greater boldness of access to the throne of grace, and in fuller communications of the free Spirit of God, than believers under the law did ordinarily partake of.

(Galatians 3:13; Galatians 1:4; Acts 26:18; Romans 8:3; Romans 8:28; 1 Corinthians 15:54-57; 2 Thessalonians 1:10; Romans 8:15; Luke 1:73-75; 1 John 4:18; Galatians 3:9, 14; John 7:38, 39; Hebrews 10:19-21)

2)   God alone is Lord of the conscience, and hath left it free from the doctrines and commandments of men which are in any thing contrary to his word, or not contained in it. So that to believe such doctrines, or obey such commands out of conscience, is to betray true liberty of conscience; and the

requiring of an implicit faith, an absolute and blind obedience, is to destroy liberty of conscience and reason also.

(James 4:12; Romans 14:4; Acts 4:19, 29; 1 Corinthians 7:23; Matthew 15:9; Colossians 2:20, 22, 23; 1 Corinthians 3:5; 2 Corinthians 1:24)

3)   They who upon pretence of Christian liberty do practice any sin, or cherish any sinful lust, as they do thereby pervert the main design of the grace of the gospel to their own destruction, so they wholly destroy the end of Christian liberty, which is, that being delivered out of the hands of all our enemies, we might serve the Lord without fear, in holiness and righeousness before Him, all the days of our lives.

(Romans 6:1, 2; Galatians 5:13; 2 Peter 2:18, 21)

Chapter 22: Of Religious Worship and the Sabbath Day

1) The light of nature shews that there is a God, who hath lordship and sovereignty over all; is just, good and doth good unto all; and is therefore to be feared, loved, praised, called upon, trusted in, and served, with all the heart and all the soul, and with all the might. But the acceptable way of worshipping the true God, is instituted by himself, and so limited by his own revealed will, that he may not be worshipped according to the imagination and devices of men, nor the suggestions of Satan, under any visible representations, or any other way not prescribed in the Holy Scriptures.

(Jeremiah 10:7; Mark 12:33; Deuteronomy 12:32; Exodus 20:4-6)

2) Religious worship is to be given to God the Father, Son, and Holy Spirit, and to him alone; not to angels, saints, or any other creatures; and since the fall, not without a mediator, nor in the mediation of any other but Christ alone.

(Matthew 4:9, 10; John 6:23; Matthew 28:19; Romans 1:25; Colossians 2:18; Revelation 19:10; John 14:6; Timothy 2:5)

3) Prayer, with thanksgiving, being one part of natural worship, is by God required of all men. But that it may be accepted, it is to be made in the name of the Son, by the help of the Spirit, according to his will; with understanding,

reverence, humility, fervency, faith, love, and perseverance; and when with others, in a known tongue.

(Psalms 95:1-7; Psalms 65:2; John 14:13, 14; Romans 8:26; 1 John 5:14; 1 Corinthians 14:16, 17)

4)   Prayer is to be made for things lawful, and for all sorts of men living, or that shall live hereafter; but not for the dead, nor for those of whom it may be known that they have sinned the sin unto death.

(1 Timothy 2:1, 2; 2 Samuel 7:29; 2 Samuel 12:21-23; 1 John 5:16)

5)   The reading of the Scriptures, preaching, and hearing the Word of God, teaching and admonishing one another in psalms, hymns, and spiritual songs, singing with grace in our hearts to the Lord; as also the administration of baptism, and the Lord's supper, are all parts of religious worship of God, to be performed in obedience to him,
with understanding, faith, reverence, and godly fear; moreover, solemn humiliation, with fastings, and thanksgivings, upon special occasions, ought to be used in an holy and religious manner.

(1 Timothy 4:13; 2 Timothy 4:2; Luke 8:18; Colossians 3:16; Ephesians 5:19; Matthew 28:19, 20; 1 Corinthians 11:26; Esther 4:16; Joel 2:12; Exodus 15:1-19, Psalms 107)

6)   Neither prayer nor any other part of religious worship, is now under the gospel, tied unto, or made more acceptable by any place in which it is performed, or towards which it is directed; but God is to be worshipped everywhere in spirit and in truth; as in private families daily, and in secret each one by himself; so more solemnly in the public assemblies,

which are not carelessly nor wilfully to be neglected or forsaken, when God by his word or providence calleth thereunto.

(John 4:21; Malachi 1:11; 1 Timothy 2:8; Acts 10:2; Matthew 6:11; Psalms 55:17; Matthew 6:6; Hebrews 10:25; Acts 2:42)

7_ As it is the law of nature, that in general a proportion of time, by God's appointment, be set apart for the worship of God, so by his Word, in a positive moral, and perpetual commandment, binding all men, in all ages, he hath particularly appointed one day in seven for a sabbath to be kept holy unto him, which from the beginning of the world to the resurrection of Christ was the last day of the week, and from the resurrection of Christ was changed into the first day of the week, which is called the Lord's day: and is to be continued to the end of the world as the Christian Sabbath, the observation of the last day of the week being abolished.

(Exodus 20:8; 1 Corinthians 16:1, 2; Acts 20:7; Revelation 1:10)

8) The sabbath is then kept holy unto the Lord, when men, after a due preparing of their hearts, and ordering their common affairs aforehand, do not only observe an holy rest all day, from their own works, words and thoughts, about their worldly employment and recreations, but are also taken up the whole time in the public and private exercises of his worship, and in the duties of necessity and mercy.

(Isaiah 58:13; Nehemiah 13:15-22; Matthew 12:1-13)

Chapter 23: Of Lawful Oaths and Vows

1) A lawful oath is a part of religious worship, wherein the person swearing in truth, righteousness, and judgement, solemnly calleth God to witness what he sweareth, and to judge him according to the truth or falseness
thereof.

(Exodus 20:7; Deuteronomy 10:20; Jeremiah 4:2; 2 Chronicles 6:22, 23)

2 The name of God only is that by which men ought to swear; and therein it is to be used, with all holy fear and reverence; therefore to swear vainly or rashly by that glorious and dreadful name, or to swear at all by any other thing, is sinful, and to be abhorred; yet as in matter of weight and moment, for confirmation of truth, and ending all strife, an oath is warranted by the word of God; so a lawful oath being imposed by lawful authority in such matters, ought to be taken.

(Matthew 5:34, 37; James 5:12; Hebrews 6:16; 2 Corinthians 1:23; Nehemiah 13:25)

3) Whosoever taketh an oath warranted by the Word of God, ought duly to consider the weightiness of so solemn an act, and therein to avouch nothing but what he knoweth to be truth; for that by rash, false, and vain oaths, the Lord is provoked, and for them this land mourns.

(Leviticus 19:12; Jeremiah 23:10)

4)   An oath is to be taken in the plain and common sense of the words, without equivocation or mental reservation.

(Psalms 24:4) (Ps. 24:4)

5)   A vow, which is not to be made to any creature, but to God alone, is to be made and performed with all religious care and faithfulness; but popish monastical vows of perpetual single life, professed poverty, and regular obedience, are so far from being degrees of higher perfection, that they are superstitious and sinful snares, in which no Christian may entangle himself.

(Psalms 76:11; Genesis 28:20-22; 1 Corinthians 7:2, 9; Ephesians 4:28; Matthew 19:11)

Chapter 24: Of the Civil Magistrate

1) God, the supreme Lord and King of all the world, hath ordained civil magistrates to be under him, over the people, for his own glory and the public good; and to this end hath armed them with the power of the sword, for defence and encouragement of them that do good, and for the punishment of evil doers.
(Romans 13:1-4)

2) It is lawful for Christians to accept and execute the office of a magistrate when called there unto; in the management whereof, as they ought especially to maintain justice and peace, according to the wholesome laws of each kingdom and commonwealth, so for that end they may lawfully now, under the New Testament wage war upon just and necessary occasions.

(2 Samuel 23:3; Psalms 82:3, 4; Luke 3:14)

3)   Civil magistrates being set up by God for the ends aforesaid; subjection, in all lawful things commanded by them, ought to be yielded by us in the Lord, not only for wrath, but for conscience sake; and we ought to make supplications and prayers for kings and all that are in authority, that under them we may live a quiet and peaceable life, in all godliness and honesty.
(Romans 13:5-7; 1 Peter 2:17; 1 Timothy 2:1, 2)

Chapter 25: Of Marriage

1)   Marriage is to be between one man and one woman; neither is it lawful for any man to have more than one wife, nor for any woman to have more than one husband at the same time.

(Genesis 2:24; Malachi 2:15; Matthew 19:5,6)

2)   Marriage was ordained for the mutual help of husband and wife, for the increase of mankind with a legitimate issue, and the preventing of uncleanness.

(Genesis 2:18; Genesis 1:28; 1 Corinthians 7:2, 9)

3)   It is lawful for all sorts of people to marry, who are able with judgment to give their consent; yet it is the duty of Christians to marry in the Lord; and therefore such as profess the true religion, should not marry with infidels, or idolaters; neither should such as are godly, be unequally yoked, by marrying with such as are wicked in their life, or maintain damnable heresy.

(Hebrews 13:4; 1 Timothy 4:3; 1 Corinthians 7:39; Nehemiah 13:25-27)

4)   Marriage ought not to be within the degrees of consanguinity or affinity, forbidden in the Word; nor can such incestuous marriages ever be made lawful, by any law of man or consent of parties, so as those persons may live together as man and wife.

(Leviticus 18; Mark 6:18; 1 Corinthians 5:1)

Chapter 26: Of the Church

1)   The catholic or universal church, which (with respect to the internal work of the Spirit and truth of grace) may be called invisible, consists of the whole number of the elect, that have been, are, or shall be gathered into one, under Christ, the head thereof; and is the spouse, the body, the fulness of him that filleth all in all.

(Hebrews 12:23; Colossians 1:18; Ephesians 1:10, 22, 23; Ephesians 5:23, 27, 32)

2)   All persons throughout the world, professing the faith of the gospel, and obedience unto God by Christ according unto it, not destroying their own profession by any errors everting the foundation, or unholiness of conversation, are and may be called visible saints; and of such ought all particular congregations to be constituted.

(1 Corinthians 1:2; Acts 11:26; Romans 1:7; Ephesians 1:20-22)

3)   The purest churches under heaven are subject to mixture and error; and some have so degenerated as to become no churches of Christ, but synagogues of Satan; nevertheless Christ always hath had, and ever shall have a kingdom in this world, to the end thereof, of such as believe in him, and make profession of his name.

(1 Corinthians 5; Revelation 2; Revelation 3; Revelation 18:2; 2 Thessalonians 2:11, 12; Matthew 16:18; Psalms 72:17; Psalm 102:28; Revelation 12:17)

4) The Lord Jesus Christ is the Head of the church, in whom, by the appointment of the Father, all power for the calling, institution, order or government of the church, is invested in a supreme and sovereign manner; neither can the Pope of Rome in any sense be head thereof, but is that antichrist, that man of sin, and son of perdition, that exalteth himself in the church against Christ, and all that is called God; whom the Lord shall destroy with the brightness of his coming.

(Colossians 1:18; Matthew 28:18-20; Ephesians 4:11, 12; 2 Thessalonians 2:2-9)

5) In the execution of this power wherewith he is so intrusted, the Lord Jesus calleth out of the world unto himself, through the ministry of his word, by his Spirit, those that are given unto him by his Father, that they may walk before him in all the ways of obedience, which he prescribeth to them in his word. Those thus called, he commandeth to walk together in particular societies, or churches, for their mutual edification, and the due performance of that public worship, which he requireth of them in the world.

(John 10:16; John 12:32; Matthew 28:20; Matthew 18:15-20)
6) The members of these churches are saints by calling, visibly manifesting and evidencing (in and by their profession and walking) their obedience unto that call of Christ; and do willingly consent to walk together, according to the appointment of Christ; giving up themselves to the Lord, and one to another, by the will of God, in professed subjection to the ordinances of the Gospel.

(Romans. 1:7; 1 Corinthians 1:2; Acts 2:41, 42; Acts 5:13, 14; 2 Corinthians 9:13)

7)   To each of these churches thus gathered, according to his mind declared in his word, he hath given all that power and authority, which is in any way needful for their carrying on that order in worship and discipline, which he hath instituted for them to observe; with commands and rules for the due and right exerting, and executing of that power.

(Matthew 18:17, 18; 1 Corinthians 5:4, 5; 1 Corinthians 5:13; 2 Corinthians 2:6-8)

8)   A particular church, gathered and completely organized according to the mind of Christ, consists of officers and members; and the officers appointed by Christ to be chosen and set apart by the church (so called and gathered), for the peculiar administration of ordinances, and execution of power or duty, which he intrusts them with, or calls them to, to be continued to the end of the world, are bishops or elders, and deacons.

(Acts 20:17, 28; Philippians 1:1)

 9.)   The way appointed by Christ for the calling of any person, fitted and gifted by the Holy Spirit, unto the office of bishop or elder in a church, is, that he be chosen thereunto by the common suffrage of the church itself; and solemnly set apart by fasting and prayer, with imposition of hands of the eldership of the church, if there be any before constituted therein; and of a deacon that he be chosen by the like suffrage, and set apart by prayer, and the like imposition of hands.

(Acts 14:23; 1 Timothy 4:14; Acts 6:3, 5, 6)

10)   The work of pastors being constantly to attend the service of Christ, in his churches, in the ministry of the word and prayer, with watching for their souls, as they that must give an account to Him; it is incumbent on the churches to whom they minister, not only to give them all due respect, but also to communicate to them of all their good things according to their ability, so as they may have a comfortable supply, without being themselves entangled in secular affairs; and may also be capable of exercising hospitality towards others; and this is required by the law of nature, and by the express order of our Lord Jesus, who hath ordained that they that preach the Gospel should live of the Gospel.

(Acts 6:4; Hebrews 13:17; 1 Timothy 5:17, 18; Galatians 6:6, 7; 2 Timothy 2:4; 1 Timothy 3:2; 1 Corinthians 9:6-14)

11)   Although it be incumbent on the bishops or pastors of the churches, to be instant in preaching the word, by way of office, yet the work of preaching the word is not so peculiarly confined to them but that others also gifted and fitted by the Holy Spirit for it, and approved and called by the church, may and ought to perform it.

(Acts 11:19-21; 1 Peter 4:10, 11)

12.)   As all believers are bound to join themselves to particular churches, when and where they have opportunity so to do; so all that are admitted unto the privileges of a church, are also under the censures and government thereof, according to the rule of Christ.

(1 Thessalonians 5:14; 2 Thessalonians 3:6, 14, 15)

13) No church members, upon any offence taken by them, having performed their duty required of them towards the person they are offended at, ought to disturb any church-order, or absent themselves from the assemblies of the church, or administration of any ordinances, upon the account of such offence at any of their fellow members, but to wait upon Christ, in the further proceeding of the church.

(Matthew 18:15-17; Ephesians 4:2, 3)

14) As each church, and all the members of it, are bound to pray continually for the good and prosperity of all the churches of Christ, in all places, and upon all occasions to further every one within the bounds of their places and callings, in the exercise of their gifts and graces, so the churches, when planted by the providence of God, so as they may enjoy opportunity and advantage for it, ought to hold communion among themselves, for their peace, increase of love, and mutual edification.

(Ephesians 6:18; Psalms 122:6; Romans 16:1, 2; 3 John 8-10)

15) In cases of difficulties or differences, either in point of doctrine or administration, wherein either the churches in general are concerned, or any one church, in their peace, union, and edification; or any member or members of any church are injured, in or by any proceedings in censures not agreeable to truth and order: it is according to the mind of Christ, that many churches holding communion together, do, by their messengers, meet to consider, and give their advice in or about that matter in difference, to be reported to all the churches concerned; howbeit these messengers assembled, are not intrusted with any church-power properly so called; or with any jurisdiction over the churches themselves, to

exercise any censures either over any churches or persons; or to impose their determination on the churches or officers.

(Acts 15:2, 4, 6, 22, 23, 25; 2 Corinthians 1:24; 1 John 4:1)

Chapter 27: Of the Communion of Saints

1)   All saints that are united to Jesus Christ, their head, by his Spirit, and faith, although they are not made thereby one person with him, have fellowship in his graces, sufferings, death, resurrection, and glory; and, being united to one another in love, they have communion in each others gifts and graces, and are obliged to the performance of such duties, public and private, in an orderly way, as do conduce to their mutual good, both in the inward and outward man.

(1 John 1:3; John 1:16; Philippians 3:10; Romans 6:5, 6; Ephesians 4:15, 16; 1 Corinthians 12:7; 1 Corinthians 3:21-23; 1 Thessalonians 5:11, 14; Romans 1:12; 1 John 3:17, 18; Galatians 6:10)

2)   Saints by profession are bound to maintain an holy fellowship and communion in the worship of God, and in performing such other spiritual services as tend to their mutual edification; as also in relieving each other in outward things according to their several abilities, and necessities; which communion, according to the rule of the gospel, though especially to be exercised by them, in the relation wherein they stand, whether in families, or churches, yet, as God offereth opportunity, is to be extended to all the household of faith, even all those who in every place call upon the name of the Lord Jesus; nevertheless their communion one with another as saints, doth not take away or infringe the title or propriety which each man hath in his goods and possessions.

(Hebrews 10:24, 25; Hebrews 3:12, 13; Acts 11:29, 30; Ephesians 6:4; 1 Corinthians 12:14-27; Acts 5:4; Ephesians 4:28)

Chapter 28: Of Baptism and the Lord's Supper

1)   Baptism and the Lord's Supper are ordinances of positive and sovereign institution, appointed by the Lord Jesus, the only lawgiver, to be continued in his church to the end of the world.

(Matthew 28:19, 20; 1 Corinthians 11:26)

2)   qualified and thereunto called, according to the commission of Christ.
(Matthew 28:19; 1 Corinthians 4:1)

Chapter 29: Of Baptism

1)   Baptism is an ordinance of the New Testament, ordained by Jesus Christ, to be unto the party baptized, a sign of his fellowship with him, in his death and resurrection; of his being engrafted into him; of remission of sins; and of giving up into God, through Jesus Christ, to live and walk in newness of life.

(Romans 6:3-5; Colossians 2;12; Galatians 3:27; Mark 1:4; Acts 22:16; Romans 6:4)

2.)   Those who do actually profess repentance towards God, faith in, and obedience to, our Lord Jesus Christ, are the only proper subjects of this ordinance.

(Mark 16:16; Acts 8:36, 37; Acts 2:41; Acts 8:12; Acts 18:8)

3)   The outward element to be used in this ordinance is water, wherein the party is to be baptized, in the name of the Father, and of the Son, and of the Holy Spirit.

(Matthew 28:19, 20; Acts 8:38)

4)   Immersion, or dipping of the person in water, is necessary to the due administration of this ordinance. (Matthew 3:16; John 3:23)

Chapter 30: Of the Lord's Supper

1)   The supper of the Lord Jesus was instituted by him the same night wherein he was betrayed, to be observed in his churches, unto the end of the world, for the perpetual remembrance, and shewing forth the sacrifice of himself in his death, confirmation of the faith of believers in all the benefits thereof, their spiritual nourishment, and growth in him, their further engagement in, and to all duties which they owe to him; and to be a bond and pledge of their communion with him, and with each other.

(1 Corinthians 11:23-26; 1 Corinthians 10:16, 17,21)

2)   In this ordinance Christ is not offered up to his Father, nor any real sacrifice made at all for remission of sin of the quick or dead, but only a memorial of that one offering up of himself by himself upon the cross, once for all; and a spiritual oblation of all possible praise unto God for the same. So that the popish sacrifice of the mass, as they call it, is most abominable, injurious to Christ's own sacrifice the alone propitiation for all the sins of the elect.
(Hebrews 9:25, 26, 28; 1 Corinthians 11:24; Matthew 26:26, 27)

3)   The Lord Jesus hath, in this ordinance, appointed his ministers to pray, and bless the elements of bread and wine, and thereby to set them apart from a common to a holy use, and to take and break the bread; to take the cup, and, they communicating also themselves, to give both to the communicants.
(1 Corinthians 11:23-26, etc.)

4)   The denial of the cup to the people, worshipping the elements, the lifting them up, or carrying them about for adoration, and reserving them for any pretended religious use, are all contrary to the nature of this ordinance, and to the institution of Christ.

(Matthew 26:26-28; Matthew 15:9; Exodus 20:4, 5)

5)   The outward elements in this ordinance, duly set apart to the use ordained by Christ, have such relation to him crucified, as that truly, although in terms used figuratively, they are sometimes called by the names of the things they represent, to wit, the body and blood of Christ, albeit, in substance and nature, they still remain truly and only bread and wine, as they were before.

(1 Corinthians 11:27; 1 Corinthians 11:26-28)

6)   That doctrine which maintains a change of the substance of bread and wine, into the substance of Christ's body and blood, commonly called transubstantiation, by consecration of a priest, or by any other way, is repugnant not to Scripture alone, but even to common sense and reason, overthroweth the nature of the ordinance, and hath been, and is, the cause of manifold superstitions, yea, of gross idolatries.

(Acts 3:21; Luke 14:6, 39; 1 Corinthians 11:24, 25)

7)   Worthy receivers, outwardly partaking of the visible elements in this ordinance, do then also inwardly by faith, really and indeed, yet not carnally and corporally, but spiritually receive, and feed upon Christ crucified, and all the benefits of his death; the body and blood of Christ being

then not corporally or carnally, but spiritually present to the faith of believers in that ordinance, as the elements themselves are to their outward senses.
(1 Corinthians 10:16; 1 Corinthians 11:23-26)

8)   All ignorant and ungodly persons, as they are unfit to enjoy communion with Christ, so are they unworthy of the Lord's table, and cannot, without great sin against him, while they remain such, partake of these holymysteries, or be admitted thereunto; yea, whosoever shall receive unworthily, are guilty of the body and blood of the Lord, eating and drinking judgment to themselves.

(2 Corinthians 6:14, 15; 1 Corinthians 11:29; Matthew 7:6)

Chapter 31: Of the State of Man after Death and Of the Resurrection of the Dead

1)   The bodies of men after death return to dust, and see corruption; but their souls, which neither die nor sleep, having an immortal subsistence, immediately return to God who gave them. The souls of the righteous being then made perfect in holiness, are received into paradise, where they are with Christ, and behold the face of God in light and glory, waiting for the full redemption of their bodies; and the souls of the wicked are cast into hell; where they remain in torment and utter darkness, reserved to the judgment of the great day; besides these two places, for souls separated from their bodies, the Scripture acknowledgeth none.

(Genesis 3:19; Acts 13:36; Ecclesiastes 12:7; Luke 23:43; 2 Corinthians 5:1, 6,8; Philippians 1:23; Hebrews 12:23; Jude 6, 7; 1 Peter 3:19; Luke 16:23, 24)

2)   At the last day, such of the saints as are found alive, shall not sleep, but be changed; and all the dead shall be raised up with the selfsame bodies, and none other; although with different qualities, which shall be united again to their souls forever.

(1 Corinthians 15:51, 52; 1 Thessalonians 4:17; Job 19:26, 27; 1 Corinthians 15:42, 43)

3)The bodies of the unjust shall, by the power of Christ, be raised to dishonour; the bodies of the just, by his Spirit, unto honour, and be made conformable to his own glorious body.

(Acts 24:15; John 5:28, 29; Philippians 3:21)

Chapter 32: Of the Last Judgment

1)   God hath appointed a day wherein he will judge the world in righteousness, by Jesus Christ; to whom all power and judgment is given of the Father; in which day, not only the apostate angels shall be judged, but likewise all persons that have lived upon the earth shall appear before the tribunal of Christ, to give an account of their thoughts, words, and deeds, and to receive according to what they have done in the body, whether good or evil.

(Acts 17:31; John 5:22, 27; 1 Corinthians 6:3; Jude 6; 2 Corinthians 5:10; Ecclesiastes 12:14; Matthew 12:36; Romans 14:10, 12; Matthew 25:32-46)

2)   The end of God's appointing this day, is for the manifestation of the glory of his mercy, in the eternal salvation of the elect; and of his justice, in the eternal damnation of the reprobate, who are wicked and disobedient; for then shall the righteous go into everlasting life, and receive that fulness of joy and glory with everlasting rewards, in the presence of the Lord; but the wicked, who know not God, and obey not the gospel of Jesus Christ, shall be cast aside into everlasting torments, and punished with everlasting destruction, from the presence of the Lord, and from the glory of his power.

(Romans 9:22, 23; Matthew 25:21, 34; 2 Timothy 4:8; Matthew 25:46; Mark 9:48; 2 Thessalonians 1:7-10)

3)   As Christ would have us to be certainly persuaded that there shall be a day of judgment, both to deter all men from

sin, and for the greater consolation of the godly in their adversity, so will he have the day unknown to men, that they may shake off all carnal security, and be always watchful, because they know not at what hour the Lord will come, and may ever be prepared to say, Come Lord Jesus; come quickly. Amen.

(2 Corinthians 5:10, 11; 2 Thessalonians 1:5-7; Mark 13:35-37; Luke 12:35-40; Revelation 22:20)

Closing Statement & Signatories

We the MINISTERS, and MESSENGERS of, and concerned for upwards of, one hundred BAPTIZED CHURCHES, in England and Wales (denying Arminianisim), being met together in London, from the third of the seventh month to the eleventh of the same, 1689, to consider of some things that might be for the glory of God, and the good of these congregations, have thought meet (for the satisfaction of all other Christians that differ from us in the point of Baptism) to recommend to their perusal the confession of our faith, which confession we own, as containing the doctrine of our faith and practice, and do desire that the members of our churches respectively do furnish themselves therewith.

Hansard Knollys, Pastor, Broken Wharf, London
William Kiffin, Pastor, Devonshire-square, London
John Harris, Pastor, Joiner's Hall, London
William Collins, Pastor, Petty France, London
Hurcules Collins, Pastor, Wapping, London
Robert Steed, Pastor, Broken Wharf, London
Leonard Harrison, Pastor, Limehouse, London
George Barret, Pastor, Mile End Green, London
Isaac Lamb, Pastor, Pennington-street, London
Richard Adams, Minister, Shad Thames, Southwark
Benjamin Keach, Pastor, Horse-lie-down, Southwark
Andrew Gifford, Pastor, Bristol, Frvars, Som. & Glouc.
Thomas Vaux, Pastor, Broadmead, Som. & Glouc.
Thomas Winnel, Pastor, Taunton, Som. & Glouc.
James Hitt, Preacher, Dalwood, Dorset
Richard Tidmarsh, Minister, Oxford City, Oxon
William Facey, Pastor, Reading, Berks

Samuel Buttall, Minister, Plymouth, Devon
Christopher Price, Minister, Abergayenny, Monmouth
Daniel Finch, Minister, Kingsworth, Herts
John Ball, Tiverton, Devon
Edmond White, Pastor, Evershall, Bedford
William Prichard, Pastor, Blaenau, Monmouth
Paul Fruin, Minister, Warwick, Warwick
Richard Ring, Pastor, Southhampton, Hants
John Tomkins, Minister, Abingdon, Berks
Toby Willes, Pastor, Bridgewater, Somerset
John Carter, Steventon, Bedford
James Webb, Devizes, Wilts
Richard Sutton, Pastor, Tring, Herts
Robert Knight, Pastor, Stukeley, Bucks
Edward Price, Pastor, Hereford City, Hereford
William Phipps, Pastor, Exon, Devon
William Hawkins, Pastor, Dimmock, Gloucester
Samuel Ewer, Pastor, Hemstead, Herts
Edward Man, Pastor, Houndsditch, London
Charles Archer, Pastor, Hock-Norton, Oxon
In the name of and on the behalf of the whole assembly.

Other books in the range:

Commentary on the Psalms

The Treasury of David Vol I: Exposition Edition

The Treasury of David Vol II: Exposition Edition

The Treasury of David Vol III: Exposition Edition

Love your Neighbour and the Cursing Psalms.

Printed in Great Britain
by Amazon

40034882R00056